EARTHMAKER'S TALES

NORTH AMERICAN INDIAN STORIES ABOUT EARTH HAPPENINGS

by

Gretchen Will Mayo

Walker and Company
New York

For my mother, Julia, whose sense of adventure
is also her gift.

First published in the United States of America in 1989
by the Walker Publishing Company, Inc.

Published simultaneously in Canada by Thomas Allen & Son
Canada, Limited, Markham, Ontario.

Library of Congress Cataloging-in-Publication Data

Mayo, Gretchen.
    Earthmaker's tales.

    Summary: A collection of North American Indian
legends about the origins of thunder, tornados, and
other weather phenomena.
    I. Indians of North America—Legends.   2. Weather—
Folklore—Juvenile literature. [1. Indians of North
America—Legends.   2. Weather—Folklore]   I. Title.
E98.F6M34   1989   398.2'6'08997   88-20515
ISBN 0-8027-6839-3
ISBN 0-8027-6840-7 (lib. bdg.)
        Printed in the United States of America

                10 9 8 7 6 5 4 3 2 1

        Book design by Laurie McBarnette

CONTENTS

earth event . . . . source tribe(s)

TRIBES
that told the
TALES

LILLOOET   CREE

HOH AND
QUILEUTE
PUGET SOUND
NISQUALLY   PLAINS CREE

                                                              MICMAC

          CHEYENNE   MENOMINI   WYANDOT
                                                  SENECA
                                                  IROQUOIS

    UTE   OTO

       UTE   KIOWA
          APACHE   CHEROKEE

INTRODUCTION

BLAM! CRASH!

With a thundering roar, the avalanche hurled down on good Algoot. Boulders smashed around him. Rocks flew in the dust. But Algoot had gathered super strength from the good spirits. He dodged the crushing boulders and threw them back at the wicked Tauquitch high on the mountain top. The people rejoiced when Algoot killed the evil creature. Because they used green wood to burn Tauquitch's body, however, his angry spirit lives on.

"It is cruel Tauquitch who makes the mountains rumble and the rocks fall from the ledges," says the old Saboba Indian storyteller.

Earth events have astonished, puzzled, terrified, and tormented people since the world began.

Tornadoes roared into the camps of our ancestors. Earthquakes rattled their bones. Storm clouds threatened destruction, and rainbows signaled calm.

From the beginning, the wise ones searched for ways to explain these things. "Why did Earthmaker bring the storm?" the Winnebago asked; and, "Who has made Earthmaker angry?" Their reasoning led to stories that helped to make sense of puzzling and frightening events.

Stories also made people laugh and forget their worries. Indians, often wonderfully creative, shared and traded their tales from tribe to tribe or with people who were not Native Americans. Because early Indians had not developed a written language, it was the European missionaries and explorers who usually recorded their stories for the first time. The tales, however, were not always written exactly as they were told. On the other hand, loving a good story, Indians wove parts of some European folktales into their own. Some legends, of course, were sacred and could never be given away or changed, even to this day.

In early days, the time and setting for storytelling was very important. Rules had to be followed, although the rules varied from tribe to tribe.

Like many other tribes, the Blackfoot insisted on telling their legends after dark and in the winter time. Stories often continued far into the night, lengthened and embellished with details and colorful descriptions. The Yavapai of central Arizona considered it dangerous to tell their stories during the summer months, when spiders and snakes might hear and bite them. They waited for storytelling until autumn, when the animals began their long sleep and couldn't listen. Then they built a good fire and sat in a circle around one of the elders of the tribe, a keeper of the old stories.

Early Native Americans lived close to the land and knew its many moods and signs. They had stories for streams they crossed, blazing sunsets, and windy storms. To them, all creation was alive with spirits, and all things were connected. From this rich treasure, born and nurtured in their lives, these tales are retold with gratitude.

EARTHQUAKE

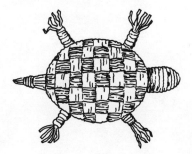

"There are too many new people!" cried the Wintu story-teller when the earth quaked. "Coyote Old Man is stretching and pulling the earth to make it larger."

Far eastward across the continent, the Yuchi Indians told about a mysterious creature of the underworld who shook the earth from time to time to see how much water remained on top.

The earthquake story of the Wyandots explained how the world began. The word Wyandot means, "They are islanders," an appropriate name for a tribe living in the land of the Great Lakes between lakes Huron, Michigan, and Superior. They traded furs with the French and the English, and their history was often linked with that of the Iroquois.

EARTH IS ON BIG TURTLE'S BACK

BACK BEFORE the world was made, Sky Woman, the beautiful daughter of Big-Chief-Above, was watching some of the people dig around a wild apple tree in the sky country. Suddenly a loud noise made the people jump back. They had broken through the floor of the sky country! The tree was sinking, making a big hole! As it dropped, the apple tree caught Sky Woman in its branches.

Falling down, down, out of the sky, the woman landed on the backs of two swans who were swimming below in the endless sea. The swans were glad to let the beautiful daughter rest on their backs after her fall, but after a while, one of them said, "This woman from the sky needs a home of her own."

So they called a council of all those living in the water.

Big Turtle had an idea. "Maybe someone can take a little mud from the tree that fell from the sky," he suggested. "Then we could make an island to float on the water."

But the tree had sunk deep into the sea. Otter, Muskrat, Beaver, and Loon all dove to find the tree but failed. Then Old Toad said that she would like to try. Old Toad was so small and ugly that everyone laughed and laughed.

3

"Quiet!" said Big Turtle. "Maybe Old Toad will do what no one else has done."

Old Toad took a deep, deep dive and was gone a long, long time. Everyone waited.

"Old Toad is too small and feeble," said Muskrat.

"Old Toad is never coming back," sighed Loon.

But little bubbles appeared on the water. Then Old Toad splashed to the surface, ready to burst, and spat out a mouthful of mud which landed right on Big Turtle's back.

Little Turtle at once began to spread the earth all around the edges of Big Turtle's shell. "Big Turtle," she said, "it looks like you have been chosen to make a home for Sky Woman!"

Big Turtle swelled with pride and the mud began to grow. When the earth became the size of a little island, Sky Woman left the swans and stepped onto Big Turtle's back, calling it her home.

Earth grew and grew until it was as large as the world is today. Sometimes Big Turtle gets a little tired holding up the earth. He moves one of his feet. He stretches the other foot. Then earth shakes and rumbles and the people shout, "Earthquake!"

FLOOD

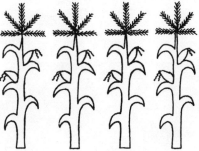

The Utes called themselves the People of the Shining Mountains. Living in the Rocky Mountain area, they told this story about Pike's Peak and a world-wide flooding of the Colorado River.

Other Native American tribes have great flood stories too. A Chitimachan tale from southern Louisiana is like many of them. All the people except a man and a woman were destroyed by a huge flood. They were saved when they made a large earthen vessel, and a dove brought them a single grain of sand from which a new land grew.

In a Papago story, the boulders on the mountain tops are the rocky forms of people who asked the Great Spirit to save them from the pain of drowning in the great flood.

THIRSTY LIZARD ENDS THE BIG FLOOD

WHEN ALL things began, earth was called the lower world because the home of the most powerful gods was above in the heavens. The less important spirits, who directed the lower world, lived below along a great river that lay across the earth like a rope, winding in the direction of the setting sun.

To carry out their wishes, the spirits of the lower world made people. But the people made endless trouble. They argued and squabbled and fought with each other until the spirits could stand it no longer.

"Why did we make these awful people?" complained the voices of the spirits across the land. "They help a little but spoil a lot!"

The spirits of the lower world ended their misery by making the Great River grow. It grew till the waters overflowed its banks, till it overran the other rivers, till it covered all the land and all the troublesome people.

There were some things of the earth, however, that the spirits loved. So before the waters had crept to every corner, they hurried about the land collecting treasures. They gathered silver and gold and sparkling rocks and even some of

7

the rich brown soil to take with them to the upper world in the sky. And they took corn, because a meal without corn was like a day without laughter.

"No earthly treasures allowed in the sky country!" roared the spirits of the upper world when the lesser spirits came.

Because they feared the gods, the spirits of the lower world dropped their great loads of earth's treasures, but secretly they hid away their corn. All the gold and silver and shining rocks fell from the heavens, landing on earth in a heap so huge that its peak rose above the deep waters. And there it sat while time rolled on.

Although the spirits of the lower world had moved to the sky country, they still kept watch over the earth. One night, as they traveled across the sky, they saw that two children had survived the great flood and were living on the heap of earthly treasures.

"See how that boy and girl gather the kernels we drop!" remarked the spirits above as they munched their ears of corn.

"Look how they plant some of the kernels in the dark, warm earth," they said later.

8

Then, after the passing of many moons, the spirits saw the boy and girl lash together corn stalks, tall and green, to make a boat.

"How clever those earth children are!" exclaimed the spirits. "How strong they have become!"

Then the spirits said to one another, "Maybe these people have earned our help. Maybe we should send them the thirsty giant."

There lived among the misty clouds a giant lizard who sipped and licked and lapped from dawn to dusk but was still always thirsty. The spirits of the lower world lead this thirsty lizard to the edge of the sky and let it dive down, down to the watery earth. With great thirsty gulps, the lizard drank and drank and drank until the heap of earthly treasures began to rise as a mountain above the sinking waters.

When Thirsty Lizard had licked the last drops of water from the land, he tried to leap high into the wet, misty clouds. But his swollen body would not rise. He fell back against the mountain of earth's treasures with a thundering crash and never moved again.

Thirsty Lizard lay there so long that his huge body turned to stone, water trickling from his scrapes and scratches. Streams bubbled from beneath the rock, tumbling down his mountainous sides to enrich the valleys below.

The people became many people. Some of them grew corn in the fertile land. some of them found the earth's treasures hidden in the mountain. They tried not to argue or squabble or fight with each other, for there was plenty for everyone. And so it was as time rolled on.

The spirits of the lower world still move across the heavens every night as groups of stars, munching their favorite food, then disappearing behind the mountains when the sun brings dawn. Sometimes the spirits are sloppy eaters. Then the kernels spill from the heavens and people below point to the sky and cry, "Look at the falling stars!"

DAYLIGHT

Many Indian legends say that the young world was always dark. Some tribal stories tell of a tricky hero who managed to light the world for the people. Sometimes Coyote was the hero. Sometimes, as in this Lillooet tale from the far Northwest, it was Raven.

In a story from the Northwest Tsimshian, the son of the Great Chief in the Sky changed the eternal darkness by wearing a mask of flaming pitch wood. He still wears it as he runs across the sky each day, bringing light to the world.

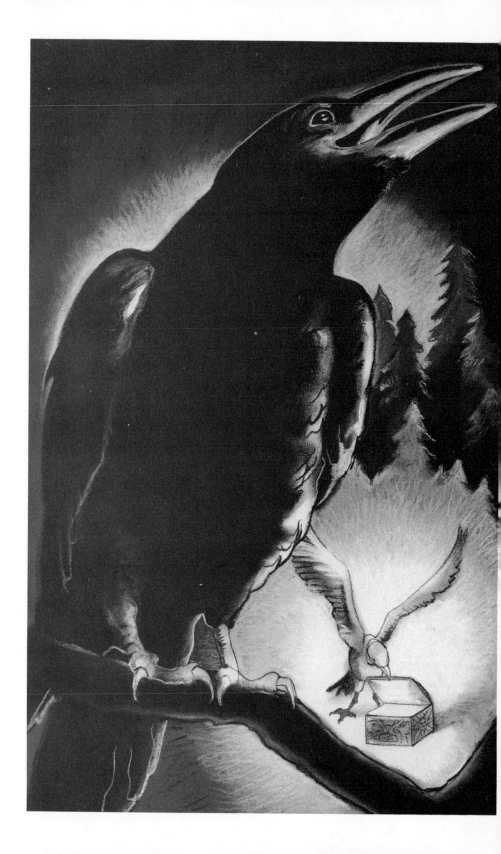

DAYLIGHT COMES AT LAST

IT WAS THE time of endless night and Black Raven set out to see what he could find. Bumping through the forest, skimming past the rocks, Raven felt his way blindly through the darkness.

Suddenly a shimmer of brilliant light flashed deep among the trees. Black Raven folded his wings and crept cautiously to find out what was going on. Then, where the trees thinned to meet the water, Raven found his old friend, Sea Gull. Sea Gull was so busy fastening shut a box that he didn't notice Raven, dark as night.

"What is it you have in your box," asked the curious Raven, surprising his friend.

"Nothing much," snapped Sea Gull. But the way he hurried off with his box made Raven certain that it held a treasure.

Raven decided to stay near Sea Gull's lodge to try to find out more. Soon Raven heard Sea Gull mumbling and fumbling in the dark. Raven crept to the door of the lodge and peered in. Sea Gull was doing something with his box. He opened the lid a little crack. Suddenly the lodge was flooded with light! Raven could see each basket, every stick

13

and every feather on Sea Gull's head. Black Raven crouched in the dark and watched Sea Gull work about his lodge without a stumble or a fumble or a bump.

"What a treasure Sea Gull has!" thought Raven. "Everyone should have this thing." But when Sea Gull was ready to sleep, Raven watched him snap down the lid of the box firmly, shutting the light back inside it, before hiding the box under his bed. "That selfish Sea Gull wants to keep his treasure all to himself," thought Raven. "Let's see what I can do to make him share it!"

Then, while Sea Gull slept soundly over his box, Raven clipped hawthorne branches from the trees around Sea Gull's lodge. Carefully, carefully, so that the long thorns wouldn't scratch him, Raven laid the branches along the path leading from Sea Gull's lodge to the water's edge. He covered the path right down to the place where Sea Gull's canoe was fastened to a stump. Then Raven untied the rope and set the canoe adrift.

"Sea Gull! Sea Gull!" shouted Raven as the canoe drifted away with the current. "Sea Gull! Your boat is floating off! Hurry!"

Sea Gull leaped from his sleep. He bumped through his doorway and bounded down the path. "OUCH! Oh! Ouch, ouch!" screeched Sea Gull. He jumped from one leg to the other right back to his house. "Raven, save my boat! My feet are full of thorns," cried Sea Gull from his doorway.

When Raven had brought back the canoe, he found Sea Gull picking the thorns from his feet.

"Let me help you," offered Raven, peering closely at Sea Gull's feet. Then, "How I wish I could see better to help my old friend," sighed Raven.

Sea Gull reached under his bed and snatched the hidden box. "Here," he moaned. "I'll give you a little light," and he opened the box a crack.

"Such big thorns!" exclaimed Raven, pulling out one, two, three. "But these little ones, I can see them hardly at all."

Groaning loudly, Sea Gull opened the box a little wider.

Raven picked and picked. "One more to go," he breathed. "Give me a little more light."

This time when Sea Gull reached for the box, Raven gave Sea Gull a little shove. The box fell open wide and all the

15

daylight escaped. Light flooded every corner of the house. It spread outside, down the path, shimmering across the water and over the hills.

"Come back! Come back!" shouted Sea Gull to his escaping treasure. He flew out the door, racing across the hills and grasping, grasping to gather back his precious Daylight. But it was too late. Daylight was spreading across the world, coming at last to all the people.

Raven, black as night, had to listen to Sea Gull's loud complaints as long as Daylight glowed. But when Daylight traveled on to the other side of the world and night came, Sea Gull yawned and fell asleep. Then Raven, black as the night, slipped into the forest to see what else he could find.

MOUNTAINS

There are many Native American tales explaining how the mountains came to be. In some, when the soft earth was being formed, Coyote ran all over leaving his footprints and digging up the mud. In those tribes living near volcanoes, the mountains were often said to be living, growing beings who became angry and even ate people.

The Apache lived in the dry plains area just east of the high mountains. In their stories, the first people came up from the underworld and found the earth inhabited by monsters. Like most tribes, the Apache believed the sun was a being with immense power. Sun's son also had special powers, but he was more like the people and was often called to help them.

BIG ELK DIGS UP THE MOUNTAINS

IN THE earliest times, all the land on earth was flat, and all the animals were gigantic monsters. Big Elk was the most terrible of all. He sprawled across the warm dry plain and gobbled up people for snacks.

The people cried out to the gods for help, so Father Sun sent his own son to see what he could do. Son of Sun crept to Big Elk's resting place to watch from behind some tall dry grass. There were no bushes or trees on the open plain, and Son of Sun wondered how he could creep closer without being seen. As he sat and pondered, Lizard, who was sunning on a rock nearby, called out, "What are you doing here, my friend?"

"My father sent me to help the people," explained the surprised son of the sun. He told Lizard how Big Elk had been gobbling the people one-by-one. "But the plain is so flat and bare," he said. "How can I get close enough to shoot Big Elk with my arrows?"

Lizard's beady eyes blinked. "The desert is home to us lizards. We sun on the rocks and rest in the shade. There are so many of us, Elk hardly notices."

"But why doesn't he gobble you like he gobbles the people?" asked Son of Sun.

"Why do I eat flies?" answered Lizard, with a flick of his long tongue. "It's just a question of taste. Maybe if you looked like a lizard, Big Elk wouldn't want you for a snack either," suggested Lizard. He wriggled out of his coat and offered it to Son of Sun.

The son of the sun squeezed one arm into Lizard's tight coat. As he was tugging at the other, the ground beneath him heaved, and up popped Gopher, knocking Son of Sun right off his feet!

"Why were you standing right over the door to my tunnel?" huffed Gopher.

"Why did you dig your door right under my feet?" answered Son of Sun.

Then Gopher peered hard at Son of Sun. "Why on earth are you wearing Lizard's coat?" she sniffed.

The son of the sun explained why he had come to the desert plain. "If Big Elk makes a meal of me, I won't be much help to the people," he said, "so Lizard gave me his coat."

"My, my, my," sighed Gopher. "To Elk you'll just look like a tasty snack in a coat that doesn't fit. But maybe I can help. If you follow my tunnel, Big Elk will never see you."

With this, Gopher dove back into her hole. Dirt flew and the ground quivered, but soon Son of Sun could see the path of a long tunnel winding across the flat plain toward the giant elk.

Gopher was gone a long time.

Even when the burrow reached the place where Big Elk rested, Gopher did not return.

"Maybe Big Elk gobbles gophers too," thought Son of Sun mournfully. Then suddenly the ground heaved again and up popped Gopher, knocking Son of Sun right off his feet.

"Why do you always stand over my door?" huffed Gopher.

"Why do you always dig your door right under my feet?" answered Son of Sun.

Then Gopher peered hard at the son of the sun. "Stop asking so many questions," she sniffed. "Go after Big Elk!"

So the son of the sun plunged into Gopher's tunnel, following it far under the dry, flat plain.

Thumpa, thumpa, THUMPA, THUMPA!

A terrible pounding overhead shook the earth around him. Son of Sun looked up and saw Elk's hide thumping right over his head. This was the beating of Big Elk's giant heart! Gopher had brought him to a spot right under the monster elk.

Without wasting a moment, the son of the sun drew his bow. Four times his arrows shot above.

But to giant Big Elk, they were like the sting of four bees. The angry elk rose up on his four tall legs to see who was stinging him and he looked right down into Gopher's tunnel at the son of the sun!

"Oh, no!" yelled Son of Sun as the enraged giant plunged

his giant antler into Gopher's tunnel. The son of the sun turned in the tunnel and ran for his life.

Furious, Big Elk gouged his way along the burrowed path after Son of Sun, ploughing up mountains of dry brown earth with his sharp antlers.

Son of Sun ran and ran. When he came to the end of the tunnel, Big Elk was right behind him. But Big Black Spider was able to help the son of the sun. He lowered a tight, strong web and blocked the charging elk so that Son of Sun could get away.

By now the monster elk was so angry that he went right on ploughing up the earth, gashing and rutting from one end of the land to the other until finally he gasped his last raging breath and dropped dead.

Son of Sun thanked Big Black Spider and the people thanked Son of Sun. From that time on, the children of fearsome Big Elk were much smaller. Father Sun ruled that his elk children would eat grasses and plants rather than people. But some things remained the same. Gopher still digs tunnels. Lizard still suns on the desert rocks. And the tall mountains ploughed by Big Elk still stand high above the flat, dry plains.

WHIRLWIND

Whirlwinds, tornadoes, and cyclones inspired exciting Native American tales. In a Blackfoot story shared by many tribes, an orphan boy rescues the people who have been devoured by Windsucker, the tornado, who was said to be a giant sucker fish. The boy kills Windsucker by doing a jumping-up dance inside the monster's belly, with a knife fastened, blade upright, on his head.

The Seneca named the tornado Dagwa Noenyent and said it was a giant rolling head that could tear the largest trees from the earth.

The ancient Kiowa Indians claim that their people are the ones who made the first tornado, and that if they spoke to it, the tornado would pass without harming them. This is their story.

THE MAKING OF WHIRLWIND

Hot SUMMER lay upon the people like a heavy moist blanket. Not a leaf moved. No whisper of a breeze lifted a strand of hair.

The people gathered around an old medicine man. "Tell us what we can do. There is hardly a breath in this hot, stuffy air," they said.

The old man sent some women to the river bank to gather red mud. When they returned he told the people to watch carefully. Then he shaped the mud into the form of an animal. It looked something like a horse, with four legs and a long tail.

"Watch me, and do what I do," said the old man to the people who were gathered around. Then the old man blew into the nostrils of the horse and it began to grow.

"Blow hard!" the old man commanded the people. They blew at the horse as hard as they could and it grew larger still until three people were needed to hold it, then ten. As they held the red mud horse, it began to stretch and twist.

"Red horse, I name you Red Wind!" called out the old man. "Now show us what you can do to cool the people."

With that, the horse tore away from the many hands that were holding it and whirled through the air, stirring it and laughing and blowing up dust.

At first the people cheered and lifted their arms to the cooling gusts. But the wind blew the feathers from their hair and the bracelets from their wrists. Red Wind twisted and jumped like a wild thing. Trees snapped as though they were twigs.

"Now look what you've done, old man!" shouted the people. "Red Wind will tear up·the earth and blow us all away!"

So the old man called out again, "Red Wind! I made you. I named you. Now I give you a home. From this time on, you will live in the sky."

Ever since then, Red Wind, the whirlwind, has lived among the black clouds. But sometimes he twists and stretches down because he likes to kick things up on earth again.

RAIN STORM

"Those lazy Cloud People don't want to work!" grumbled the Zia Indians whenever thunder and lightning came before the rain. They said the rumble of the Thunders' flapping wings and the flaming arrows shot by the Lightning People were meant to frighten the Cloud People into making rain for the parched earth.

The hero of this Seneca story about rain storms is a woman. Among the Seneca, women had great power. Chiefs and tribal council members were nominated by women, and the women removed them if they misbehaved. Women were said to prevent some wars.

The Seneca were the largest tribe in the Iroquois Confederacy. They lived in the area of northern New York State where Lake Ontario and Lake Erie come together.

BRAVE GIRL AND THE STORM MONSTER

JIJOGWEH, the evil monster bird, made the storms and lived on the blood of humans.

The terrified people never knew when the wandering, blood-thirsty, evil bird would swoop down out of the clouds. They crept about carefully and watched the skies, but Jijogweh was as cunning as he was swift and powerful. Sweeping his gigantic wings down along the lakes and rivers, he made the waters churn and hiss until clouds boiled up to hide him. Then with one touch of his wings, the clouds turned angry black, pouring dreadful rain and slimy snakes on the poor frightened people.

There were some people who found the courage to shoot their arrows at Jijogweh when he flew at them, but none of them lived to tell of it. If his poison breath hadn't killed them first, their arrows fell back broken as Jijogweh attacked. And should even one feather fall from his wing, the blood drops turned to rock, smashing those still alive below.

One night as all the people slept, a dream message came to a strong young woman named Brave Girl. She should shape a strong bow from the wood of an ash tree, stringing it with her own long black hair. The message added that

29

if she also feathered her arrows with down from the breast of a young eagle, she could destroy the terrifying monster bird.

The young woman didn't waste time thinking of what might happen to her. Brave Girl left at dawn, climbing a high rocky cliff to an eagle's nest. When she dropped tasty bits of meat into the baby birds' open mouths, they let her pluck a handful of down. Hurrying home, the young woman made her bow and arrows just as the dream message had told her. Then she found the medicine man, who placed around her neck a pouch of sacred tobacco, asking the good spirits to help her and giving her some sacred words.

Feeling the protection of the good spirits and trusting her strong bow and arrows, the young woman waited for dark. Then she went alone to the edge of the water and crawled under some sheltering grape vines. All night she watched for the monster bird, but no living thing stirred.

"The evil one is busy somewhere else," Brave Girl thought. Suddenly, as she was gathering her things to leave, there was a terrible shriek. Looking up, she saw the giant wings of the evil bird circling above. How huge Jijogweh was!

How long was his sharp beak! But quickly she reached for her arrow.

"Aaaaeee!" wailed Brave Girl, staring at the arrow shaft which hung like a wilted blade of grass in her hand. "The wet night air has taken the life from my arrows!"

But the strong young woman would not let herself lose courage. "Good spirits of the night, be my friends!" Brave Girl called, grasping her medicine pouch. Then, as Jijogweh loomed closer, she drew another arrow, whispering the powerful words taught to her by the medicine man. This time her arrow lay firm against her bow. Shooting straight and true, Brave Girl pierced the wicked heart of the blood-thirsty bird.

The monster fell, its wings beating the air wildly and thrashing the water until it foamed. Then as the evil bird sank beneath the surface forever, a flock of gulls rose like a cloud from the water, hovered a moment, and flew away.

The storytellers say that Jijogweh had eaten the gulls in his terrible hunger and they were released at last by his death. Jijogweh's ghost still haunts the clouds but he cannot suck the blood of humans. Now, whenever Jijogweh makes a storm, the gulls fly up to warn the people. It's their way of thanking Brave Girl.

THUNDER AND LIGHTNING

Many Indian tribes have a thunder story. In some, Thunder is a powerful messenger of the Almighty, often in the form of an enormous bird. The Thunderbird of the Assiniboin teaches its children by making a loud noise which they repeat over and over.

The Thompson River Indians have a funny story about Thunder. An envious Thunder noticed that Mosquito was very fat and wondered where he got so much to eat. Mosquito was afraid that if he told the truth, Thunder would eat up all the people. "I suck on trees," Mosquito answered. So today Thunder shoots trees with his bolts of lightning rather than shooting people.

In this story from Puget Sound tribes, Thunder and Lightning were once two brothers who roamed the mountains.

HOW THUNDER
AND LIGHTNING
CAME

ENUMCLAW and Kapoonis were brothers who were fine hunters but wanted to become something more. These two brothers were often away from the village for many moons, hunting wild game, drying the meat, and hiding it to use later. But their travels had another purpose because each searched for a guardian spirit that would make him a great medicine man.

Kapoonis tried to find his guardian spirit in a vision. Every morning and every night he took baths in the river so he might be worthy of a powerful vision. That's how he found a fire spirit so powerful that he was able to throw flames from one bank of the river to the other.

Meanwhile Enumclaw grew strong too. In the mountains he practiced tossing stones from one peak to another, making sharp cracking sounds. Sometimes he threw the stones against rocks to call his younger brother or send him signals. Each day Enumclaw threw larger stones. Each day the cracks grew louder.

When he saw people crossing the mountains, Enumclaw threw rocks at the nearby peaks warning his brother that someone was near. But now the terrible noise hurt the ears

35

of the people and made them run home. "Enumclaw frightens the largest birds and makes them fly so fast their wings make loud rumbles!" cried the people. "And Kapoonis throws arrows of fire from peak to peak!"

Enumclaw and Kapoonis did not know the people were frightened. To them, it was a game to test their power.

One night the two brothers sat on a rocky ridge facing the setting sun. "Look Kapoonis," said his brother. "There is a great white rock across the river. I will throw stones on the left side of the rock so hard that the ridge along the river will fall."

"Sounds like fun!" said Kapoonis. "I'll flash my bolts of fire to the right."

Enumclaw threw his stones as hard as he could and Kapoonis hurled out great bolts of flame, igniting the sky and sending the people to hide and cover their ears. Afterwards, there was nothing left of the ridge along the river.

From above the peaks, the Great Spirit watched the brothers playing their games and wrecking the land. "It is too dangerous for humans to have so much power," said the Great Spirit. So he made Enumclaw and Kapoonis thunder and lightning and gave them a new home far above the people.

RAINBOW

"The Rain's Hat"; "The Great Spirit's Fishing Line"; "Strong-Medicine-to-Drive-Away-Rain"; "Cloud-Boy's Sky Path." These were names given to the rainbow by different tribes across the country. To the Zia, rainbows were paths that only war heroes were allowed to travel. But the Yuchi said the gods had stretched a rainbow across the sky to prevent any more rain from falling.

This story from the Hoh and Quileute tribes is about a mysterious rainbow woman who lived on the other side of the ocean. The Hoh and Quileute live on the Olympic Peninsula in the state of Washington.

THE HUNTER AND RAINBOW WOMAN

O NE FINE morning long ago, a hunter shot a duck with a newly made arrow. The arrow did not harm the duck, but settled deep in her feathers. When she flew away, the arrow flew with her.

To the hunter, this was a very special arrow, so he followed the duck, hoping to get it back. All day he pursued the duck until he was completely lost, but still he went on. He followed the duck to the far side of the ocean. When finally he reached the opposite shore, there was a surprise waiting. The duck had changed into a giant woman!

"Now I have you!" screamed the giant as she snatched the hunter. "I've been waiting to catch a new husband, and here you are!" Grabbing a hank of the hunter's hair, the giantess pulled him along beside her. On their way to her house, they passed a neighbor, who whispered a few words of caution to the hunter.

"Watch out! Tonight she'll kill you and eat you, just like the others!"

Late that night when the hunter thought the giant was asleep, he escaped. He dashed through the trees, over the hills and along the water until once more he was lost. He could hear the giant woman's thundering footsteps in the distance. Suddenly a beautiful woman dressed in cloth of many colors appeared in his path.

Stopping to catch his breath, the hunter asked, "Who are you?"

"I am Rainbow Woman," said the stranger. "Why are you running so fast?"

"Don't you feel the earth tremble?" said the hunter. "Those are the footsteps of an evil giant who wants to kill me."

"Then I can help you," replied Rainbow Woman. "Run on ahead. I'll follow in a moment."

When Rainbow Woman caught up with the hunter, they could hear the giant woman thumping down the path, shaking all the trees as she rumbled along. Then, WOOMP! and everything was silent.

"What did you do?" asked the hunter.

"I set a trap," said Rainbow Woman. "Now, come along and rest at my house," she said, for already she loved him.

So the hunter went off with the beautiful Rainbow Woman and by morning he had fallen in love too.

The hunter married Rainbow Woman and after a while, they had a child. But one morning the hunter took his bow and arrows, as he often did, and went hunting. When he had not returned by afternoon, Rainbow Woman went out to look for him, but she could not find him. To this day, he has not returned.

Rainbow Woman knows her husband has just lost his way again, so she keeps watch faithfully. Sometimes she climbs into the sky so she can see better to search the land. When we see a double rainbow, we know her child is searching with her, too.

HOT SPRINGS

Hot springs, where thermal waters bubble up from the ground or stand in warm pools, drew Native Americans from great distances. Sometimes hundreds gathered at such a spot to bathe in the healing waters. The Indians traded horses, fruits, and handmade things while they camped. They traded stories too. The Sioux said the Underground People heated the waters so that flowers and healing herbs would grow all year long.

There are many hot springs in the land of the Utes. Their story about the origin of the springs also explains how these once peaceful hunters and seed-gatherers came to battle with the Cheyenne, Arapaho, and other tribes.

SMOKING WATERS

A LONG time ago, the people of the mountains lived in peace. The forests and streams fed them so that they never slept hungry. They were content with their brothers and sisters. They were safe in the shelter of the mountains.

In time, a restless young man named Many Feathers became chief and things began to change. Many Feathers fished the streams he had fished before and wished for new ones. He looked at the sheltering mountain slopes and felt imprisoned. Then when the old ones told tales of people beyond the mountains, Many Feathers dreamed he wore the robe of a great chief, a leader of many warriors.

"Our elders say the people beyond the mountains have more horses than they have children," Many Feathers exclaimed one day. "If we fight them, their horses can be ours."

Some listened.

"Great battles make great heroes. A brave warrior walks in honor on every path," he said.

And others listened.

So Many Feathers called a council in the shadow of the mountains and told the old ones to teach them the war

dances of their ancestors. One of the old ones, a medicine man named Smoking Waters, refused.

"We are happy here," said the old man, and his arm swept forward, tracing the circle of surrounding mountains. "The birds of the sky and creatures of the land are our brothers here," he said. "We have what we need. We need nothing more."

"You are afraid, old man!" laughed Many Feathers, mocking him. "Stay in the lodge with the women and children!"

"My brother speaks with the voice of the North Wind," responded Smoking Waters gravely. "As the North Wind brings snow and winter's death, so you will bring sorrow and death to our people."

"I will bring power to our people!" shouted Many Feathers.

Then Many Feathers turned to face his people. "This old man is like the timid rabbit who runs before he looks," he cried. "Beat the drums! Dance the war dances! We will make ourselves heroes!"

Many Feathers' words made the hearts of his people pound. They cheered and beat the drums. When they left

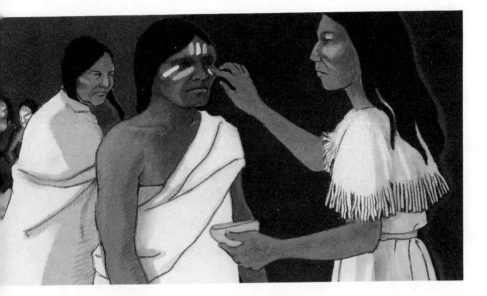

the council, the people laughed at the old medicine man and drove him from the tribe.

The people danced the forgotten war dances. They tightened their bows. They painted their faces and dressed their hair with feathers, bone and thongs of hide. Then the fathers, sons, and brothers marched beyond the shining mountains to war.

Many of them died.

Later, deep in the mountains, where his lonely campfire burned on the bank of a stream, Smoking Waters saw his people in a vision. But where were the hunters, he wondered. Where had the fathers gone? Children were crying for food. The women were thin and bent with sickness. Drums beat out the death chants. The people of the mountains no longer sang their joyful songs.

As Smoking Waters wept for his people, his tears mingled with the waters of the mountain stream. He cried for the ones who had died and for those who suffered. He grieved until the sadness was bigger than life, and then the old medicine man died.

But Smoking Waters' love for his people lived on in the

fire he had built. It burned on without dying through the nights and the years. It burns even today, warming the waters of the streams that flow within the mountains. Now, as it was then, the mountain hot springs soothe the sick and the weary and heal the wounded. They are Smoking Waters' gift of love and peace to all the people.

SNOW

A great serpent spirit coils his back against the ice dome of the sky. With its sharp scales rubbing the ice, it scrapes and scratches, making snow dust fall. This was how ancient Shoshone storytellers explained the coming of snow.

In many other Indian tales, it was Cold-Maker or North Wind who brought the blizzards. The Blackfoot, though, said that Father Sun gave a warning sign to the people. "When Sun paints both his cheeks, snow storms are coming," said their elders. Today we call those bright spots in the cloudy sky *sun dogs.*

The Menominee and the Micmac Indians each had stories about the fierce winter spirit who made the people miserable. Their stories were similar and make the tale that follows.

SNOWMAKER TORMENTS THE PEOPLE

ONE TERRIBLE winter Snowmaker made the icy winds howl so that even the wolves ran away to a warmer place. The people heaped their fires with wood and chips, but Snowmaker hurled the blizzards against their lodges. Soon all the fuel was gone.

When the people of the tribe went out to gather sticks and branches, cruel Snowmaker stung the noses of the children and then their ears. He breathed on the women's hands until they were raw and stiff. He piled drifts so high that some men who dared to search deep in the forest for wood never returned.

One man of the tribe, Blue Feather, stumbled home on feet like chunks of ice. "Snowmaker has grown too big! He tosses the people around and laughs!" he complained to his wife.

"Don't say those things about Snowmaker," cried his wife. "Haven't we suffered enough? Snowmaker will only heap more snow on our path and make the winds blow longer."

So Blue Feather kept his silence. But he thought, "Snowmaker needs to be taught a lesson." Then, while the icy

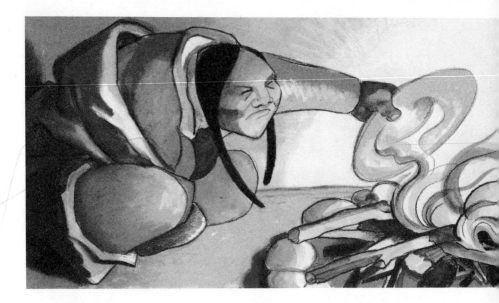

gales roared outside, Blue Feather chiseled and carved from his largest log a wooden bowl.

In time the sun grew warmer and Snowmaker grew quiet. Little by little he shrank away from the village. Soon nothing was left of Snowmaker but a patch of icy snow hidden in the cool, shadowy forest. This was when Blue Feather took out his wooden bowl. Before Snowmaker could vanish completely, Blue Feather scooped the last of the snow into his bowl, then he carried it to a rock and let the hot sun beat down, melting the snow.

"Ha! Cruel Snowmaker!" he shouted. "You only torment the people when Father Sun is gone. Now you are not so big. Now I laugh at you and I am not afraid!"

But a chill little wind came out of the north at just that moment, winding itself around Blue Feather and overturning the bowl. "Just wait!" it whispered. "Just wait!"

When autumn came again, Blue Feather worked harder than anyone else in the village. His firewood heaped as high as his lodge. He had many furs. But he did more. He saved the fat of the animals he killed and instead of using it for food he made oil, which he kept in his wooden bowl. Then,

50

when the cold winds tore the last leaf from the forest
branches, Blue Feather knew Snowmaker would come back
to settle their fight, so he built a lodge for himself away
from his wife and children.

The days grew shorter and Blue Feather saw signs that
Snowmaker was preparing to attack. The ground turned
cold and hard. The grasses withered. But when Snowmaker
froze his meat and berries, Blue Feather used his fire to
warm them.

Then one day, Father Sun was gone and Snowmaker
came into the village, swirling snow and wailing his cruel
laughter. Blue Feather pulled on his warm moccasins and
gathered his fur robes around him.

Snowmaker heaped snow on the village all day, but he
waited until night when the people were asleep to sweep
boldly into Blue Feather's lodge.

Snowmaker spread a white rug for himself and sat down.
He blew his icy breath, laughing, and made Blue Feather
shiver. He shook his great snowy head, killing the flames
of Blue Feather's fire.

"I have never been so frozen," thought Blue Feather as

he felt the cold squeeze the life from him. "Maybe if I go to sleep, Snowmaker will leave." But Blue Feather called upon his last bit of strength and reached out instead for the oil he had saved, flinging it on the dying fire. The flames roared alive, leaping to the smoke hole, lighting up the lodge.

While new life came to Blue Feather, Snowmaker shrank away from the flames, sweating and gasping. When Blue Feather let his fur robes drop from his shoulders and threw more oil on his fire, Snowmaker crouched against the wall of the lodge, sweat pouring from him in a stream.

"You have beaten me," hissed Snowmaker in a small weak voice. Then the shrunken bully stumbled out of Blue Feather's lodge, leaving only a wet trail behind him.

Snowmaker still comes again and again to torment the people, but because of Blue Feather he has lost some of his power, and the people are strong. When the hills turn golden, the children gather wood. The women store away the dried meat and the berries. And the men bring home warm furs, saving the oil to make their winter fires burn brightly.

WAHCONDA—ECLIPSE, EARTHQUAKE, THUNDER AND LIGHTNING

Like many Native Americans living west of the Mississippi River, the Otos spoke of the sun as a powerful spirit who lived beyond the Rocky Mountains. Some called this spirit Wahconda. It was Wahconda who ordered the seasons and commanded the storms.

The Otos' tale about a sad and angry Wahconda is also a love story and there is a wedding. Marriage customs differed from tribe to tribe. Often marriages were arranged by parents, who also chose the partner. In other tribes, a young person was free to ask the one he or she loved.

WAHCONDA MAKES THE EARTH SHAKE

LITTLE BLACK Bear, head chief and greatest warrior of the Oto nation, had ten sons but only one daughter. His daughter was the most beautiful of all the maidens of the land. Her long, glossy hair was black as a raven's wing. She had the footstep of a cautious deer. And she was as kind as she was beautiful. Her name was Star-Flower.

By the time she reached her seventeenth summer Star-Flower could have chosen any young warrior of the tribe for a husband. The young men hunted blue heron and the Spirit Bird to give Star-Flower red, yellow, or blue feathers for her hair. They made bracelets for her wrists and earrings of bone and shell.

In the month of green corn, a young stranger, tall and straight as a hickory tree, rode into the village of the Otos and everything changed. Guiding his white horse slowly through the village, he went straight to the lodge of Little Black Bear. He left his horse to feed on the grass and entered the lodge of the chief.

"Who are you and why have you come here?" asked Little Black Bear, who was resting on a bed of skins.

The young man, whose hair was dressed with the feathers of the song sparrow, said he had come from the lodge of his father among the Mountains of the Setting Sun. "I am the son of Wahconda, the Great Being," he told the astonished chief.

"Then Wahconda must have a message for me," said Little Black Bear with wonder in his eyes.

"I come with my father's blessing to ask for Star-Flower. From high in the mountain home of my father I have watched her. Star-Flower's beauty brings a song to my heart. But I have come to love her even more because she is so kind."

"If Wahconda's Son takes my daughter away to the land of the setting sun, he will take the sunlight from my day!" cried Little Black Bear.

"Wahconda tells you this," answered the handsome stranger. "When Little Black Bear's eyes dim with the mists of age and his knees are feeble, he can join his daughter and her little ones in the land of ever-sunny skies. Then Little Black Bear will be as filled with joy as the bird of morning."

"How will I know that Wahconda has said this," asked Little Black Bear.

"I will give these signs," answered Wahconda's Son. "When morning comes, my father will show himself in a cloudless sky, but in the time it takes to draw a breath, the earth and sky will plunge into darkness. Then you will hear the voice of my father. And last, he will open his eyes and you will see the power of his glance."

Little Black Bear drew back and gasped at these boastful words. But he answered, "If these things are done, Wahconda has indeed spoken and my daughter is yours."

It was quickly told around the village that Wahconda's Son had come from his father's lodge to make beautiful Star-Flower his wife. The people whispered that in the morning the handsome stranger would prove that he spoke

56

the truth. They were afraid of the signs promised by Wah-conda's Son.

When morning came, the young man kept his word. The sun entered a cloudless sky, but in the space of one breath, the earth and sky turned dark as the darkest night. In another breath, thunder crashed from the heavens, knocking the people to their knees. The thunder rumbled and rolled in darkness and then stopped. The people waited. The sun appeared again, sending darkness back to the cave of night. Then, from a cloudless, sunny sky, great bolts of lightning slashed at the earth, splitting trees and crushing rocks. Then it was done.

The people, whose faces were buried in their arms, looked up. This must indeed be the son of the Great Being!

So Star-Flower became the wife of Wahconda's Son. When the feasting was over and the last song had been sung, the people walked with their beloved Star-Flower and her new husband to the edge of the forest. Little Black Bear prayed that peace would be always between Wah-conda's Son and the people of Star-Flower. Then, as the people waved farewell, Star-Flower mounted the white horse behind her husband and the two rode away.

Two months passed. On a night more beautiful and still than Little Black Bear could remember, the Otos had come to the lodge of their chief to dance and feast. The people had just sat down to eat the good things of the land when suddenly the earth beneath them began to move like stormy waters. On every side the earth rumbled and rattled.

The people tried to run from the lodge, but they rolled about like a canoe in a storm. Inside they stumbled and fell. Outside they heard the crashing of trees and rocks, the screams of animals, the snap of cracking earth.

It ended, but throughout the long night, the ground shuddered and rolled. The people lay in the dark sleepless, their bodies tensed and ready to jump.

When morning came, the Otos could not believe what they saw. Trees everywhere were uprooted and broken. Small streams had vanished. In some places the earth had sunk and water filled the hollows. Rocky cliffs stood where none had been and all around were gaping cracks in the ground. Every bird was silent.

"What has happened to make the gods so angry," wondered the Otos fearfully.

Little Black Bear called together the elders and the medicine men. "Why have the great spirits done this?" he asked. But they shook their heads because no one had an answer.

Then, after the passing of three suns, Little Black Bear awoke in the morning to hear weeping outside his lodge and found his beloved daughter, Star-Flower. But how sad she looked! Her long black hair hung dirty and tangled. Her cheeks were hollow and her knees bent weakly.

"What do I see!" cried Little Black Bear, gathering his daughter in his strong arms. "Star-Flower, where have you been?"

"I come from the valley this side of the mountains," she answered in a voice so tired.

"Where is Wahconda's Son?"

"Dead, dead!" wept Star-Flower. Then she told her father that before reaching the Mountains of the Setting Sun, she and Wahconda's son had been met by a pale stranger who had shot her husband with bolts from a smoking spear.

The chief moaned because now he understood many things.

"Wahconda's Son has been killed. The Great Being is angry with the children of the earth," said Little Black Bear at last. "He shakes the earth to punish us."

Chief Little Black Bear called his people together to begin the songs of death and mourning. They painted their faces and their hair to show their sadness. They sang the low sorrowful songs of lovers torn apart. They cried out the anger of the Great Being whose son was killed by the children of earth. Then they asked the great Wahconda to heal the land of the beautiful Star-Flower, whom his son had loved.

Wahconda soon called Star-Flower away from her people to join his son in the land of the spirits. But Star-Flower returned often to look upon the place where she had been born, and it was she who healed the wounded earth. Her soft breath came as sweet spring breezes to make flowers grow across the land. Trees sprouted in the warm soil and birds sang again in the morning air.

Sometimes in the season of growing things, Star-Flower comes by moonlight to gather flowers while the Otos sleep. Then her warm breath scatters the seeds so that new flowers will cover the hills and her people will be happy again.

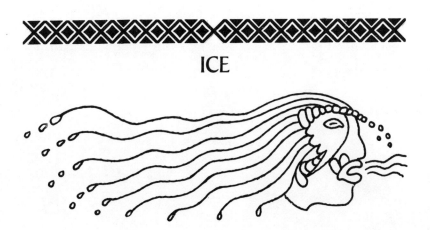

ICE

Ice Man, Cold-Bringer, Winter Man were all names Native Americans gave to the fierce spirit of the cold months. In a Sanpoil legend, Northern Lights was the ruler of the cold. He had five cold sons who each went out in their turn to bring the winter kill farther and farther south.

There was coal in the mountains of the Cherokee Indians. It may be that their Ice Man story, shared here, is about a fire that burned deep into a vein of coal, threatening to go on forever.

The Cherokee farmed in the southern Appalachian Mountains until many were forced to sell their lands and move west to the area we know as Oklahoma. Others remain in their mountain homeland to this day.

ICE MAN PUTS OUT THE BIG FIRE

ONE FALL, the people started a big fire to burn off the underbrush. A tall poplar tree caught fire and burned long after the people had gone. It burned the branches and the trunk and when there was nothing left, the fire settled in roots and burned a hole in the ground.

The next day men passed pots of water from the river to the hole. The women threw in dirt and rocks. But still the fire burned until the small hole in the ground became a huge hole.

The people peered deep into the hole. "Will this fire eat up the whole world?" they asked fearfully.

Then one of the elders spoke. "Far north lives fierce Ice Man, who sends our frozen season. Maybe cold will kill the fire." So some of the people marched the long way north to ask for Ice Man's help. Creeping cautiously to his ice house, they found a small man with white hair hanging to the ground.

"Can this little man help us with such a big fire?" they wondered.

"Yes, yes! I can help you," he exclaimed, quickly unbraiding his long hair. Then he took his hair in one hand and whipped it across the other. At once a cold wind began to blow. He struck his hand with his hair a second time and a light rain fell.

"A little rain won't kill that fire," cried the people. So Ice Man shook his hair fiercely and raindrops turned to sleet. With another shake, hailstones pelted the ground, bouncing around the people's feet.

"Go back now," Ice Man commanded. "When you are home, I will take care of your fire."

So the people returned home and found the others still watching helplessly.

The next morning as everyone stood before the glowing pit, a cold wind swept down from the north. The people shivered and shook, but the wind only made the flames blaze higher. Then a light rain began to fall. But the fire laughed and hissed and threw up clouds of smoky steam.

Now Ice Man was angry. He mixed sleet with the heavy rain and shook down snow. But the fire hissed louder. When the flames had eaten up the snow, Ice Man whipped his hair and threw cold winds at the flames until hail covered the fire and filled the hole. The people shivered and cried in their lodges as the wind became a whirlwind, driving rain and sleet into the ground and finally killing the last of the burning embers.

When it was over, the people crept back to the place where fire had been burning up the world and found instead a deep and beautiful lake.

Ice Man blows down from the north from time to time to make sure greedy Fire was really killed. But some of the people say that on quiet days, from deep in the lake, comes the faint sound of embers still crackling.

VOLCANO

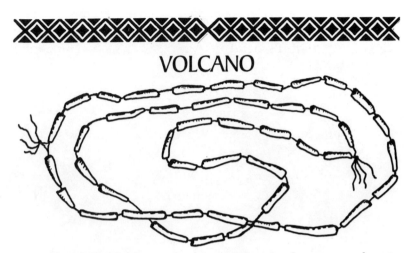

The Nisqually Indians lived in a land of active volcanic mountains which are now called the Cascade Range. Mt. Rainier, Mt. Adams, and Mt. St. Helens are among them. In early times, many of the Indians living there would not climb the mountains above the snow line. They said avalanches were angry warnings sent by mountain spirits. They have many tales giving reasons for the rumblings within the mountains.

One story is about a volcano who was really a greedy monster. She grew and grew, loudly eating all the plants, people, rocks, and trees around her. Finally, she ate so much that she burst in a violent eruption.

THE MOUNTAIN ROARS!

RUNNING ELK and his wife always had food in the pot and meat drying on the racks because he was the most cunning hunter and fisherman in the land. He always found the secret pools of fresh water where fish hid and elk came to drink. He spotted scrapes on the bark of trees or bits of fur in the branches when he chased game in the forest. But Running Elk took no pleasure in his skills. When he hunted, he searched for ways to gather more wealth.

"Bring me haiqua!" he growled when hungry people asked him to share his bounty. "When you bring haiqua, you can have some bits of dried salmon." More than anything, Running Elk loved haiqua, the little shells that were used for money.

When tracking deer, Running Elk did not see the meadow filled with yellow flowers. When he fished the sparkling streams, he did not sing with the rippling waters. He thought about haiqua. And always, he asked his spirit helper, Moosmoos, the elk, to guide him to more haiqua. "Show me waters with haiqua as thick as pebbles on the shore," he begged.

One night Moosmoos, tired of Running Elk's nagging,

told him there were great stores of haiqua hidden under three rocks at the top of the mountain. Running Elk wasted no more time sleeping. He fashioned climbing picks from the antlers of an elk. He packed his bag with dried salmon. And before dawn had chased night to the other side of the world, Running Elk was working his way up the mountain.

For two nights and a day Running Elk climbed without resting, so eager was he to find his precious haiqua. When he reached the top Running Elk did not look at the sun-painted clouds beneath him. He did not hear the singing of the wind. He saw only the three big rocks that Moosmoos had foretold. Running Elk went to one shaped like the head of an elk and began at once to dig. Moosmoos was right! After digging until the sun had crossed the heavens, Running Elk managed to overturn the rock and found more haiqua than he could count.

He began at once to string the shells on sinew. When he had more shells strung than he could loop around his neck, he wound them around his arms and his waist.

Finally Running Elk muttered, "One more haiqua will weight me to the ground, and I have more than I need to be a rich man." So he hurried down the mountain to begin enjoying his great wealth.

But greedy Running Elk had forgotten the spirits of the mountain. He spoke no thanks for their generous gift. He left no offering of thanks. He filled his thoughts with counting his strands of haiqua.

Suddenly, the mountain began to shake. Pebbles danced. Rocks tumbled. The ground beneath Running Elk's feet trembled and heaved. Then the mountain opened its mouth and roared, spitting out fire and hurling boulders down the cliffs. Molten rocks fell like rain. Snow melted into torrents, flooding through the forests below. "Haiqua, haiqua, haiqua," hissed the hot breath of the mountain as Running Elk fled for his life. "Haiqua, haiqua."

Running Elk tore the strands of shells from his arms and waist. He flung the loops away from his shoulders and tried to hide. But the storm spirits picked him up and dashed him down the mountainside. Running Elk lay at the bottom as though asleep.

Many winters fell on the mountain before Running Elk awakened. When finally he opened his eyes, he found himself an old man, his white hair falling to his waist. He looked around and saw he was in a place he faintly remembered, a beautiful meadow carpeted with yellow flowers and filled with the songs of birds. Squinting to peer across the field, he saw smoke rising from the fires of his village. "Where is my wife?" thought Running Elk, shaking sleep from his head. He rose and stumbled away to look for the lodge he had left.

He found his wife at the edge of the village, bent over her cooking fire. "Why, you are an old woman!" blurted Running Elk when she turned at his footfall.

"Just as you are old," said his wife. "Many long winters I waited for your return," and she showed him the long row of notches on their lodge pole. Then Running Elk's wife scooped some hot camas roots from her cooking fire. "Thirty winters is a long time to wait for your dinner," she said. "Are you hungry?"

Running Elk took the roots gladly and ate them with a little dried salmon. He shared what was left with the people who gathered to look at him. "Tomorrow I will bring fresh salmon for everyone," he promised without a thought of payment, because back on the mountain he had lost his love for haiqua. "With a little luck, we'll feast on elk meat, too!" And then he laughed because suddenly the sharing made him happy.

Running Elk became a medicine man and spent the rest of his days in honor. Now he marveled at the beauty of the wildflowers. He thanked brother elk who gave his life to feed the people. And every morning he asked Mountain That Roars to speak softly.

SHINING WATERS

The lakes and rivers gave food, transportation, fresh water, and often protection. So the Winnebagos gave the water spirits sacred offerings. But to early American Indians, the waters were also mysterious. Why did they turn violent? What were the whirlpools? What lurked in the dark depths? These were questions that made for good stories.

The Cherokee told tales of a monster leech, and they prayed to friendly water-dwellers to help them catch fish. The Micmac Indians of Nova Scotia had tales of a monster snake that made the waters churn and boil. In California the Shasta Indians said vicious water dogs drowned people in the whirlpools. It was the Iroquois, though, who gave us this tale of peaceful waters.

WHY THE GREAT SPIRIT MADE THE WATERS LIKE MIRRORS

WHEN THE Great Spirit made the earth, he put water in the valleys to form lakes and he sent streams flowing down the hills to make rivers. But he did not give water the power to shine back the reflection of his children's faces. That happened later, after the men of war came.

The people had been living together peacefully beside a great river. One day a group of young hunters dashed into their village shouting that many strangers were approaching beyond the river. "They carry bows twice the size of the tallest man," shouted the hunters. "Some are holding spears thick as trees with huge sharpened stones bound to the end."

"The evil spirits of the forest have befuddled you!" said the chief. And the elders nodded. But they sent out scouts and runners nevertheless.

In a short time the scouts returned, shouting that the strange warriors were coming indeed and they were as countless as the pebbles on the river bank.

"We have always lived in peace!" cried the frightened people. "How can we fight these men of war?" They sent their medicine men to the sacred cave to ask the Great Spirit what to do.

When the Great Spirit spoke, he told his children not to be afraid for he would protect those who kept peace in their hearts. He told them to build fires at nightfall all along the river banks.

The people gathered branches and twigs, piling them as the Great Spirit had directed. When night came, they lighted the bonfires. Then they shrank back in wonder when they saw as many fires burning in the water as were flaming on the shore.

The army of strange warriors saw the fires burning in the water, too. "Those people have terrible magic in their power," they said to one another. "Maybe we shouldn't attack till morning."

When dawn came the strange warriors felt brave again and plunged into the river to begin their attack on the sleeping village. But the Great Spirit was watching. He called down the storm spirits from the mountain tops. They whipped and churned the waters until the attackers disappeared. Not one was left to tell of it.

When the storm spirits had finished and gone back to the mountain tops, the peaceful children of the Great Spirit took their canoes out on the river. The water was clear and shining. The people looked into it and saw their own faces reflected in the water. Above them they saw the smiling face of the Great Spirit. When the Great Spirit saw what pleasure the beautiful shining waters gave to his peaceful children, he decided never to change them.

FOG

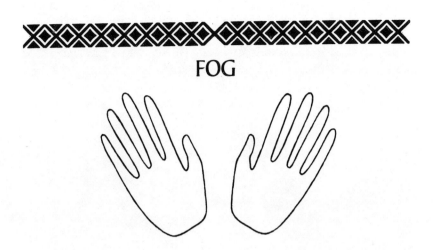

In a Tsimshian story about fog, the daughter of the Great Chief In The Sky dips her long skirts into the waters of the sky country. When she wrings out her clothing over her father's fire, she makes a cooling fog to block the heat of the sun and refresh the hot, tired people below.

The Cree Indians had their own story about fog and the spirit of evil. The Crees originally lived in the Canadian forests, but bands of them moved south onto the plains and became buffalo hunters. There they are known as the Plains Cree.

WHEN FOG COMES DRIFTING

EVIL-DOER hated Makusue. It was all because Makusue, the old Cree medicine man, had taught his people not to follow Evil-Doer's wicked ways. Makusue, beloved by the Great Spirit, could call down rain from the clouds. He foretold the storms and tempests. He knew all the herbs and roots and barks to cure diseases. This wisdom and strength came to Makusue because he worshiped the Great Spirit with love in his heart.

Makusue taught the people the signs in the sky. He showed them where to find the herbs that cured their pains. And when he spoke, the people also learned about love and kindness.

Evil-Doer never missed a chance to upset Makusue's plans. If Makusue went to dig roots, Evil-Doer made the earth freeze. If Makusue set out to cross the lake, the wind would blow and rain would drench him before he left the shore.

But Makusue laughed at the evil spirit's tricks. When Evil-Doer made the storms rage, Makusue shouted that the winds were like the breathing of a fly. If Evil-Doer hid in the shadows, Makusue pointed and said, "Evil-Doer hides because he is so ugly!" Like two cross dogs fighting over a bone, Evil-Doer and Makusue fought for the people.

Evil-Doer was losing his followers. "No one comes to the Land of Wicked Souls!" he raged. "Where are the bad people for me to torment?" So Evil-Doer went to the Great Spirit to complain.

"You agreed," whined Evil-Doer, "that if good people came to you when they died, I would have the bad people."

"And I have kept that agreement," said the Great Spirit.

"But the Land of Wicked Souls is almost empty!" shouted Evil-Doer. "It's all because of that old medicine man, Makusue. When he cures their pains, he teaches them kindness. When he shares his food, he teaches them love. Now no one follows my way. No one belongs to me!"

"Well," said the Great Spirit thoughtfully, "it is true that my faithful servant, Makusue, has taught the people to be honest and kind. When the people die they are good people. But even good people have sometimes been bad," sighed the Great Spirit.

"Yes, yes! Even the best were sometimes a little bad!" agreed Evil-Doer eagerly.

"I will offer a new agreement," said the Great Spirit at last. "Because even good people can do a little bad, all people will come to you when they die, but only for three suns and three sleeps. After that, good people will come to me. You can keep the bad people."

"Sounds great to me!" said Evil-Doer gleefully. "I'll get my fires ready to welcome them!"

"One more thing," called the Great Spirit after Evil-Doer. "You must agree to kindle your fires only in the low and marshy grounds where they will not spread."

"Oh, yes, yes," muttered Evil-Doer impatiently. Then Evil-Doer hurried away to tell Makusue about the new

bargain.

"This cannot be!" cried Makusue. He put on his sacred robes, painted his long hair with clay and went to the foot of the Mountain of Thunder, where he called out to the Great Spirit. "Oh, Great Spirit," he cried, "I am old and have served long to bring my people to you. When they die they are good people, yet you will hand them over to the torments of Evil-Doer!"

"The agreement is fair," answered the Great Spirit, "for all people are not all-good and Evil-Doer must be paid for his accomplishments."

"But let the punishment for my good people be softened," prayed Makusue. "Evil-Doer is strong and they are sometimes weak."

The Great Spirit listened to the medicine man's pleas. "What you say is true," spoke the Great Spirit. "Because you have served me long and well, Makusue, I will soften the punishment. Evil-Doer will have the people for three suns and three sleeps when they die, as I agreed. But I will give them a different form when they die so that Evil-Doer cannot hurt them with his torments. I will give them the form of the misty fogs. It is well."

So it is.

The fog that lies in the lowlands is the spirit form of those who have died. They are on their way to the happy hunting grounds of the Great Spirit . . . unless, of course, they have been friends of Evil-Doer!

BEAVER BRINGS THE END OF THE WORLD

The Cheyenne say that the father of all is a snow white beaver living far to the north. And that it is Beaver who will bring the end of the world.

Father Beaver is the guardian of a great post on which the earth rests. When the people make Father Beaver angry, he gnaws on the post. The support is already partly eaten away. Some day the people will anger Father Beaver once too often and he will gnaw the last little bit. Then the earth will fall and the people will be no more.

WHERE THE TALES BEGAN

1. **EARTH IS ON BIG TURTLE'S BACK** was recorded in 1899 by William E. Connelley who was adopted by Wyandots of the Deer Clan and given the name, Rainbow.

2. **THIRSTY LIZARD ENDS THE BIG FLOOD** was included in a collection of legends about the Pikes Peak area by Ernest Whitney in 1892.

3. **DAYLIGHT COMES AT LAST** is part of a longer tale told in 1912 by James A. Teit for the *Journal of American Folklore.*

4. **BIG ELK DIGS UP THE MOUNTAINS** was told by Laforia, a very old Jicarilla Apache woman, whose grandson, Gunsi, interpreted it for Frank Russell in 1898.

5. **THE MAKING OF WHIRLWIND** was inspired in part by a Kiowa tale, briefly recorded by Elsie Clews Parsons in 1929, which was told by Old Man Slim, who received both the story and his name from his mother's grandfather.

6. **BRAVE GIRL AND THE STORM MONSTER** is one of many Iroquois legends written by Harriet Maxwell Converse in 1908.

7. **HOW THUNDER AND LIGHTNING CAME** was told by Henry Sicade to Hermann Haeberlin and published in the *Tacoma Evening News* in 1916.

8. **THE HUNTER AND RAINBOW WOMAN**, told by Klekabuk, was

recorded some time between 1905 and 1909 by Albert B. Reagan while he was a government agent for the Hoh and Quileute tribes.

9. **SMOKING WATERS** was found in an 1873 edition of Out West magazine in an article by William N. Byers.

10. **SNOWMAKER TORMENTS THE PEOPLE** was suggested by a legend from the Menominee tribes told in 1892 by Walter James Hoffmann, M.D., and by a similar Micmac tale told by Marion Foster Washburne in 1915.

11. **WAHCONDA MAKES THE EARTH SHAKE** was adapted from a legend told by James Athearn Jones in 1830.

12. **ICE MAN PUTS OUT THE BIG FIRE** was given by Swimmer, a greatly respected storyteller, to James Mooney, who recorded it in 1897.

13. **THE MOUNTAIN ROARS!** includes retold sections of a long legend related by Hamitchou to Theodore Winthrop at Fort Nisqually and published for the first time in 1863.

14. **WHY THE GREAT SPIRIT MADE THE WATERS LIKE MIRRORS** is retold from a story written by William W. Canfield in 1902.

15. **WHEN FOG COMES DRIFTING** is based on a story related in "Tales of an Indian Camp" by James Athearn Jones, an explorer, in 1830.

16. **BEAVER BRINGS THE END OF THE WORLD** is briefly mentioned in an article by A. L. Kroeber which appeared in a 1900 edition of the *Journal of American Folklore*.

GLOSSARY

Appalachian Mountains–the major mountain system in eastern United States, extending from Canada to Alabama

Avalanche–a mass of snow, ice, or earth falling down a mountain side

Beaver–a large rodent with a broad, flat tail. With its long front teeth, the beaver cuts trees and uses them to build dams and dens along streams

Black spider–a web-spinning arachnid

Blizzard–a violent snowstorm with high winds

Buffalo–North American bison

Camas root–the edible bulb of the camas plant, a member of the lily family

Canoe–a long, narrow boat made of wood, bark or hides. Canoes made from birchbark were lightweight and easy for one or a few to carry. Some dugout canoes, made from huge logs, could carry more than fifty people.

Cascade Range–a chain of forested mountains in western United States extending from British Columbia to Northern California

Chips–small pieces of wood or dried buffalo dung used for fuel

Coal–a black mineral which burns and is used for fuel

Council–a group of leaders who make decisions for the tribe

Coyote–a swift, cunning mammal, related to, but smaller than, the wolf

Cyclone–a storm with high winds circulating around a center of low pressure

85

Down–soft, fine feathers

Duck–a waterfowl with a flat bill and webbed feet

Eagle–a large, powerful bird of prey with sharp vision

Earthquake–shaking of the earth's surface, usually caused by movement of underground rock.

Elders–the older people of a tribe

Elk–the largest member of the deer family. Older males have large antlers with many tines.

Ember–a smoldering piece of wood or coal

Fog–a fine mist or cloud near the ground

Gopher–a brownish burrowing rodent with large front teeth and long front claws

Guardian Spirit–a supernatural being that was a personal spiritual helper and the source of a man's or a woman's power

Gull–a web-footed water bird found near all oceans and many lakes

Iroquois Confederacy–a league of five Native American nations including Mohawk, Oneida, Onondaga, Cayuga and Seneca, and joined later by the Tuscaroras

Hailstones–pellets of frozen rain

Hawthorne–a shrub or small tree with long thorns

Herb–a plant used as medicine or flavoring

Heron–a large wading bird with long legs and broad wings

Hickory–a tree of the walnut family with hard, tough wood

Leech–a segmented worm which usually feeds on blood. Most live in water.

Lizard–a long-tailed, four-legged reptile, most commonly found in warm climates

Loon–a diving water bird with a laughing call

Marsh–swampy, wet land

Medicine Man–a tribe member said to have supernatural healing powers

Mississippi River–large river of central United States, flowing south from Northern Minnesota to the Gulf of Mexico

Moccasins–soft, leather slippers

Mosquito–a small insect with long legs. The female feeds on the blood of animals.

Muskrat–a brown rodent found in ponds, streams and marshes

Northwest Coast–an area of the North American Pacific Coast extending northward from Northern California to Alaska

Northern Lights–the aurora borealis. Luminous forms of color in the night sky.

Otter–a water mammal of the weasel family with a slender body and thick, brown fur

Pikes Peak–a 14,100-foot mountain in the front range of the Rocky Mountains in Colorado

Pitch–resin found in evergreen trees

Plain–an expanse of level land

Poplar–a deciduous tree of the willow family having lightweight, soft wood

Puget Sound–a huge bay between the Olympic Peninsula and the Cascade Mountains in Washington State

Rabbit–a small, short-tailed mammal common in North America, with hind legs adapted to running and jumping

Rainbow–an arc of colors of the spectrum appearing in the sky when sunlight shines through rain or mist

Raven–a glossy black bird of the crow family with a croaking call

Salmon–a fish. The Pacific Salmon is known for the long journeys it makes upstream to its breeding grounds.

Serpent–a snake

Sinew–dried fibers of an animal tendon

Sleet–partly frozen rain or a mixture of rain and snow

Smoke hole–an opening in the lodge or structure through which smoke escapes

Smoking spear–a gun

Sucker fish–a freshwater fish with a mouth adapted for sucking

Swan–a large water bird with a long, slender neck

Thermal waters–water which is warmer than the surrounding air and which flows or spouts from deep in the ground where rocks are hot

Thong–a narrow strip of leather

Toad–an amphibian similar to the frog, generally found in moist places

Tornado–a dark, destructive, funnel-shaped cloud with violent rotating air, extending from a cloud mass to the earth

Tunnel–an underground passage

Turtle–a reptile with a hard shell covering a soft body

Volcano–a vent on the earth's surface through which lava, gases and rocks are discharged from below. A cone-shaped mountain of these materials may form around the vent.

Warrior–a person experienced in fighting wars

Whirlwind–a violently revolving current of forward-moving air

Wolf–a flesh-eating mammal related to the dog

SOURCES OF INFORMATION

Wm. N. Byers, INDIAN LEGENDS, Out West Magazine, July, 1873; Wm. N. Canfield, THE LEGENDS OF THE IROQUOIS, 1902, reprint by Ira Friedman, 1971; Harriet Maxwell Converse, MYTHS AND LEGENDS OF THE NEW YORK IROQUOIS, Education Department Bulletin #437, Dec. 15, 1908, University of the State of New York; Ellen Russell Emerson, INDIAN MYTHS, Boston, 1884; James Athearn Jones, TALES OF AN INDIAN CAMP, London, 1830; Walter McClintock, THE OLD NORTH TRAIL, London, 1910; Marion Foster Washburne, INDIAN LEGENDS, Rand McNally and Co., Chicago, 1915; Ernest Whitney, M.A., LEGENDS OF THE PIKES PEAK REGION, Denver, 1892; Theodore Winthrop, THE CANOE AND SADDLE, Boston, 1893; Reports from the Bureau of American Ethnology, Volumes 14, 19, and 31; Journal of American Folklore, Volumes 11, 12, 13, 25, 37, and 46; University of California Publications in American Archaeology, Volume 4; Colorado Historical Society, Denver; Milwaukee County Public Museum.

Very special thanks are due Dr. Alice B. Kehoe, anthropologist and author of NORTH AMERICAN INDIANS: A COMPREHENSIVE ACCOUNT, and Judy Turner of the Milwaukee County Public Museum library.